Learning Social Skills
A Conversation Workbook

This Workbook Belongs To:

_____

_____

_____

For more information, visit www.Do2Learn.com

Author: The Do2Learn Team

ISBN: 978-1-60323-009-4 (Paperback)

Introduction

Conversation is a key to human interaction. It is important to be able to express your ideas and opinions so that other people can better understand your actions and your needs.

You also should be able to understand the ideas and opinions of others or they will usually not help you get what you want, and may even avoid being around or make fun of you.

Conversations can involve a set of complex rules. This workbook explains some of the more basic ones and gives you visual guides and blank pages that you can fill in to practice the conversation tips with others.

Topics include:

Why Have Conversations?

Sometimes people feel like being alone. While this is okay from time to time, there are reasons for being with other people and appropriate conversations are part of the interaction you will be expected to handle when that happens. Examples where conversations are expected might be at mealtimes, in the classroom, or even just coming home and being asked a question by your mother or roommate.

If you don't like a conversation or situation where you are expected to participate, keep in mind that it will only last for a while. Try to plan a 'reward' for yourself (watching a movie, surfing the internet, playing a video game, etc) after you do a good job participating. After you become comfortable with conversations, you will find it easier to be around, share with and enjoy the company of others. Most people find conversations fun and you may also once you master them.

You can also help erase anxiety about conversations by making a plan for how to start, carry on, and end them. You can do this by answering some important questions about what might happen and preparing possible responses. The tips in this workbook are to help you feel more comfortable and prepared for conversations with many people and in a variety of situations.

Some Conversations are Not Optional ...

To improve your social abilities and increase your social opportunities, it is important to be able to have conversations with other people. There are times at home or with family that you will be expected to talk to other people.

List below three times at **home** or with **family** that you will be expected to carry on a conversation:

There are times at **school** or **work** when you will be expected to converse with others. List below three times when your teachers, classmates, supervisors, or co-workers will expect you to engage in conversation:

Remember that sometimes even when you don't feel like participating in something, it is required and is the right thing to do.

Prepare for Conversation...

Use this handy T-Chart to help prepare for specific situations in which you will need to have conversations with other people.

Overview: _Kara's Mom will be driving us both to band practice after school this week._

Questions about the Situation	Answers
When & Where will this conversation be happening?	_In the car after school._
Who will I have to have a conversation with?	_I will have to talk to both Kara and her Mom._
How long will it last?	_Probably about 20 minutes._
How will I be expected to participate in this conversation?	_Kara's Mom will ask me how my day was. I will tell her that it was fun because we played soccer in gym class._

Some conversations are more difficult than others. Write down a small reward that you will allow yourself to have if you successfully complete the conversational task.

Reward: _I will get to play an extra 10 minutes of my favorite video game before dinner._

Prepare for Conversation...

Use this handy T-Chart to help prepare for specific situations in which you will need to have conversations with other people.

Overview: _____

_____

_____

Questions about the Situation	Answers
When & Where will this conversation be happening?	
Who will I have to have a conversation with?	
How long will it last?	
How will I be expected to participate in this conversation?	

Some conversations are more difficult than others. Write down a small reward that you will allow yourself to have if you successfully complete the conversational task.

Reward: _____

_____

_____

Prepare for Conversation...

Use this handy T-Chart to help prepare for specific situations in which you will need to have conversations with other people.

Overview: _____

_____

Questions about the Situation	Answers
When & Where will this conversation be happening?	
Who will I have to have a conversation with?	
How long will it last?	
How will I be expected to participate in this conversation?	

Some conversations are more difficult than others. Write down a small reward that you will allow yourself to have if you successfully complete the conversational task.

Reward: _____

_____

Prepare for Conversation...

Use this handy T-Chart to help prepare for specific situations in which you will need to have conversations with other people.

Overview: _____

_____

_____

Questions about the Situation	Answers
When & Where will this conversation be happening?	
Who will I have to have a conversation with?	
How long will it last?	
How will I be expected to participate in this conversation?	

Some conversations are more difficult than others. Write down a small reward that you will allow yourself to have if you successfully complete the conversational task.

Reward: _____

_____

② Who Should You Talk To?

The type of conversation you have will vary depending on your **relationship** to the other person. Your **family** is the group of people you live with and are closest to. You can pretty much talk about anything with your family.

While you do not choose your family, you can choose many other people in your life. The friends you have can come from many different places such as school, work, or even your neighborhood. Each of these friends can be a different level of relationship, and therefore involve a different kind of conversation. While a classmate may be your best friend and you feel that you can speak about anything with him/her, other friends may not be as close.

It is safer to be less personal about your feelings in conversations to all but your closest friends or family members. Most people only have one or two people they tell everything to, while they may have many more casual friends with whom they talk about more general things. A close friend can be someone you can tell anything to while an acquaintance may simply be a classmate that you ask to share a homework assignment.

The relationship chart on the following pages will allow you to pinpoint the people in YOUR life that you are closest to. This will help you decide what subjects you can safely discuss with each group.

Your Relationship Circle

It is important to understand where the different people in your life fit into the relationship circle to understand what is appropriate to talk about with each. Fill in the Relationship chart below with the names of the people in your life and where you think they fit. Start at the center with the people who are closest to you...

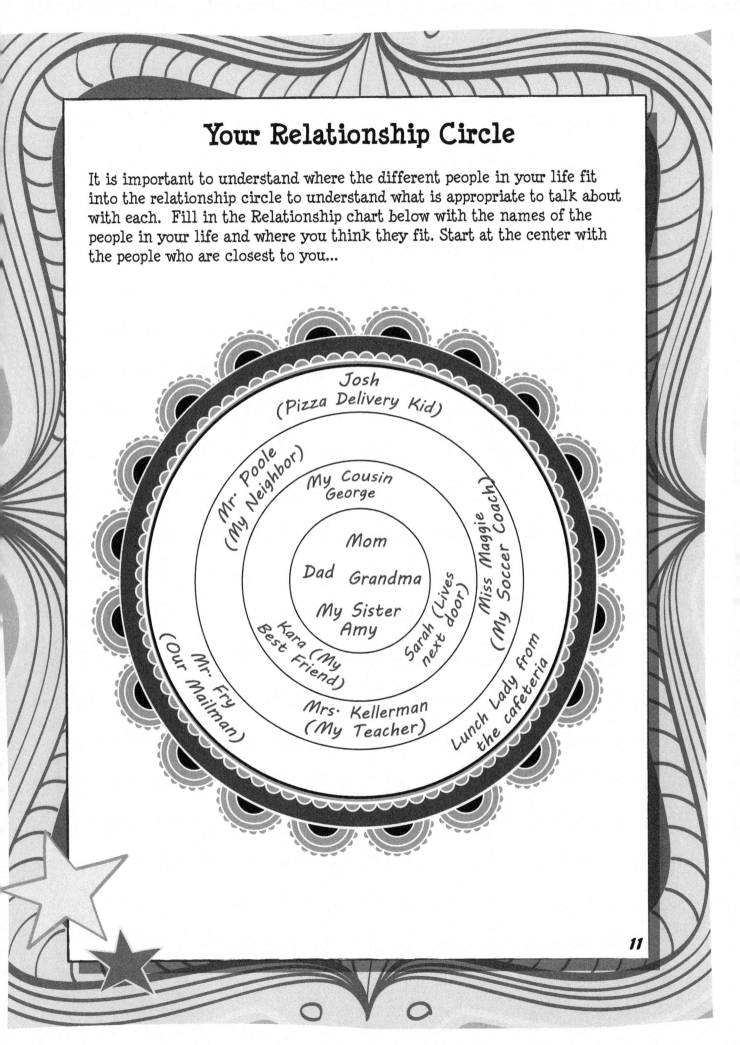

Josh
(Pizza Delivery Kid)

Mr. Poole
(My Neighbor)

My Cousin
George

Mom

Dad   Grandma

My Sister
Amy

Kara (My
Best Friend)

Sarah (Lives
next door)

Miss Maggie
(My Soccer Coach)

Mr. Fry
(Our Mailman)

Mrs. Kellerman
(My Teacher)

Lunch Lady from
the cafeteria

Your Relationship Circle

It is important to understand where the different people in your life fit into the relationship circle to understand what is appropriate to talk about with each. Fill in the Relationship chart below with the names of the people in your life and where you think they fit. Start at the center with the people who are closest to you...

Your Relationship Circle

It is important to understand where the different people in your life fit into the relationship circle to understand what is appropriate to talk about with each. Fill in the Relationship chart below with the names of the people in your life and where you think they fit. Start at the center with the people who are closest to you...

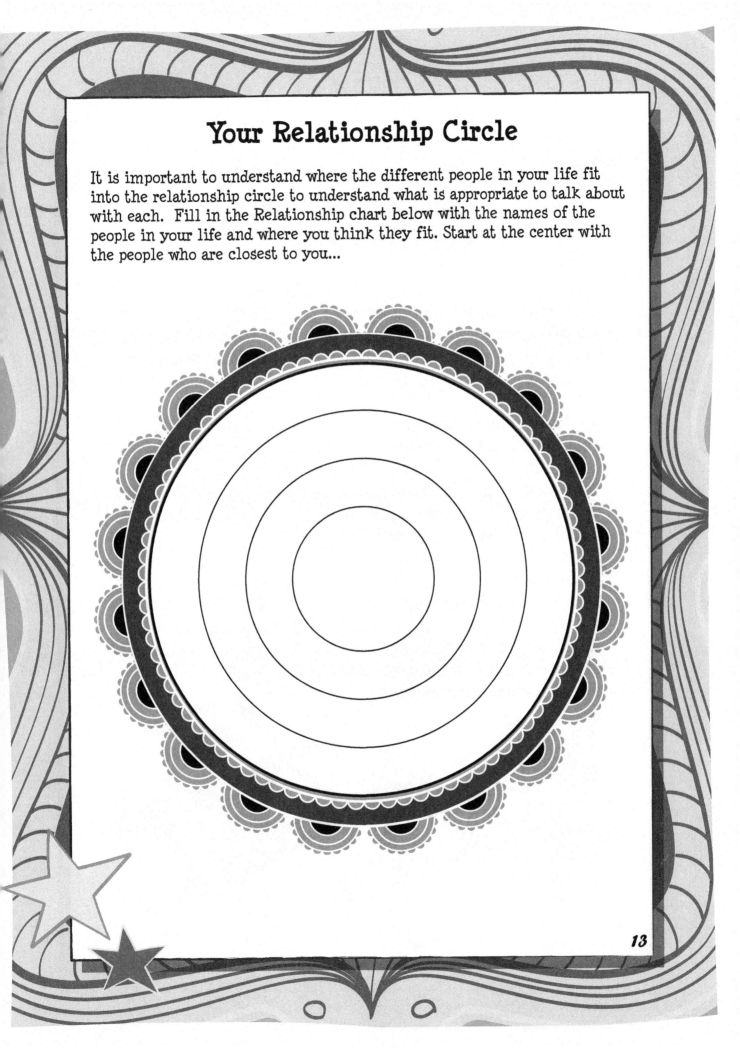

Appropriate Topics of Conversation

When it comes to making conversation, one of the biggest challenges is figuring out what to talk about. As you have already learned, a conversation you have with your friend will often be very different than a conversation you have with your teacher.

Typically, topics of conversation should be things that both people are interested in discussing. It's hard to engage in conversation about topics that you don't find interesting, and alternately, the other person won't really enjoy having a conversation with you about something that he/she isn't interested in also.

A topic that works is often something that everyone has in common. For example, a good topic of conversation with a classmate would be something related to school. When speaking with a sales clerk at a store, a good topic of conversation would be to discuss the details of the items you are purchasing.

Topic choice can be confusing since it may be fine to talk about a particular topic with one person but it may be inappropriate to have the same discussion with someone else. For example, you may be able to express to a friend the anger that you feel about being required to do chores at home, but you should not do this with a sales clerk when you are buying groceries.

The right conversation can also be affected by the time and place. Talking about the TV show you watched last night when you should be studying for a test in the library is an example of the wrong time and place for that discussion. Talking about your dog's illness at your best friend's birthday party would also be considered the wrong place and time for that topic.

In general, good conversations take into consideration **WHO** you are talking with as well as **WHERE** and **WHEN** the conversation takes place. While this may sound tricky, the activities on the following pages will help you figure out how to have an appropriate conversation with the people you see every day.

With time and practice, you'll be conversing like a pro!

My Groups...

The family members you live with make up your primary family group. Friends that you hang out with make up another group. Other groups could include friends from work, teachers at school, and waiters at your favorite restaurant. Make a list of the people in your groups...

Friends

Family Members

Teachers

Can you think of one more group?

Topics of Conversation by Groups

Group	Appropriate Topics	NOT Appropriate Topics
Family Members	-school -friends -chores	I can talk about anything with my family
Friends	-games -interests -homework	-how much money my dad makes
Teachers	-rules -local activities	-religion -politics -money
Store Clerks	-weather -purchase items	-personal information -family problems

Topics of Conversation by Groups

Group	Appropriate Topics	NOT Appropriate Topics

Topics of Conversation by Groups

Group	Appropriate Topics	NOT Appropriate Topics

Topics of Conversation by Groups

Group	Appropriate Topics	NOT Appropriate Topics

Topics of Conversation by Groups

Group	Appropriate Topics	NOT Appropriate Topics

TOPICS OF CONVERSATION ACTIVITY

Instructions:

1 List a person described in the first box and which group he/she is in.

2 Think about the types of things that would be appropriate to talk about with this particular person.

3 List an appropriate topic in each of the three Topic boxes below the person's name.

Here's an Example:

Family Member:

Aunt Pat

Topic:

What I'm studying in Geography Class

Topic:

My dog Bo and the new tricks I've taught him

Topic:

What I'm going to do this weekend

Appropriate Topics of Conversation

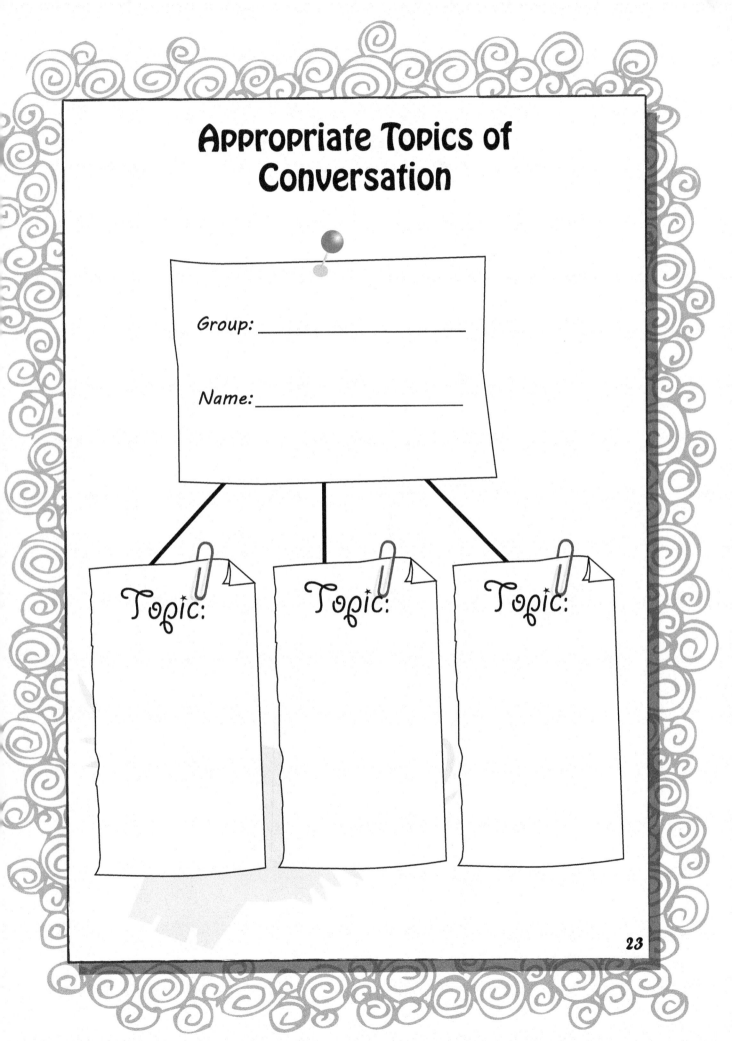

Group: _____

Name: _____

Topic:

Topic:

Topic:

Appropriate Topics of Conversation

Group: _____

Name: _____

Topic:

Topic:

Topic:

Appropriate Topics of Conversation

Group: _____

Name: _____

Topic:

Topic:

Topic:

Person, Time & Place Tree

Fill in a person you know and the time & place you will be seeing them below the tree. Then write three subjects and specific things you can discuss on each subject in the spaces provided.

Their Trip
-How long was it?
-Where did they drive through?

Activities
-Dance class
-Learning the clarinet

School
-Grades
-Social Science Class

Person: _Grandma_

Time & Place: _Thanksgiving Day visit at our house_

Person, Time & Place Tree

Fill in a person you know and the time & place you will be seeing them below the tree. Then write three subjects and specific things you can discuss on each subject in the spaces provided.

Person:_____

Time & Place: _____

Person, Time & Place Tree

Fill in a person you know and the time & place you will be seeing them below the tree. Then write three subjects and specific things you can discuss on each subject in the spaces provided.

Person:_____

Time & Place: _____

Person, Time & Place Tree

Fill in a person you know and the time & place you will be seeing them below the tree. Then write three subjects and specific things you can discuss on each subject in the spaces provided.

Person: _____

Time & Place: _____

29

 Starting a Conversation

Sometimes starting a conversation with someone can be very difficult. It can be hard to know how to begin with someone to whom you would like to talk or with someone when you are expected to carry on a conversation. It can also make you feel anxious or nervous because you might be worried about what to say and how to say it or how to respond once the conversation begins.

To help make starting conversations a little easier, it can be helpful to have some standard ways to begin a dialogue. It is important to make sure that your conversation starter is appropriate for the level of familiarity that you have with the person you will be talking to.

For instance, you wouldn't want to start a conversation with your school principal by asking a question about his private life outside of school. That would be inappropriate. However, you could start a conversation with him by asking him how he is doing that day or something related to his interests.

If you know he is a football fan, you could certainly ask him if he saw the game on television last night. That would seem very appropriate for the relationship that you have with him as principal/student and shows that you like him enough to remember that he likes football.

Make sure to practice conversation starters that are comfortable for you to remember and say to others. For instance, don't practice saying to a friend, "Hello __(Person's Name)__, how are you today?" if you would rather say, "Hey ____(Person's Name)____, What's up?"

There are many ways to begin a conversation with others and it is important for you to choose the ones that work best for you and are appropriate for the person and the time and place.

Using the groups and people from the Topics of Conversation forms you filled in before, make up some Starter Conversation words in the following forms.

Conversation Starters

In the top row, write down three possible conversation starters. List the people in each group that it would be appropriate to use with, and cross out the groups that would be inappropriate for that conversation starter.

Starters ⟋ Group	"Dude, whatssssu-uuup?"	"Good Morning, (Person's Name), how are you today?"	"Hi (Person's Name), what are you doing?"
Family	✗	-Mom -Dad -Grandma	-Mom -Dad -Sister -Brother
Friends	-Michael -Kevin	✗ Note- I could say this to my friends, but it is a little too formal···	-Caitlin -Kerry -Dan -Juanita
Authority Figures	✗	-Mrs. Berry -Mr. Storm -Bus Driver (Mr. Poole)	-Coach Peterson
Acquaintances	✗	-Neighbors (Mrs. Fields) -Postman	-Neighbor kid (Robby)

32

Conversation Starters

In the top row, write down three possible conversation starters. List the people in each group that it would be appropriate to use with, and cross out the groups that would be inappropriate for that conversation starter.

Starters			
Group			

Conversation Starters

In the top row, write down three possible conversation starters. List the people in each group that it would be appropriate to use with, and cross out the groups that would be inappropriate for that conversation starter.

Group \ Starters			

Conversation Starters

In the top row, write down three possible conversation starters. List the people in each group that it would be appropriate to use with, and cross out the groups that would be inappropriate for that conversation starter.

Group \ Starters			

Starter Sentence Worksheet

Person: _Ryan (Cousin)_
Time & Place: _Spending the weekend at our house_

What are some of his/her interests or topics you want to talk about?

- Movies
- Video Games
- We both play soccer

Write a sample starter sentence:

"Hey, Ryan, have you gotten to play the new Batman game that just got released on the X-box?"

Person: _Mr. Peterson (Boss)_
Time & Place: _First day on the job_

What are some of his/her interests or topics you want to talk about?

- What time you should arrive at work
- Work Responsibilities
- How excited you are to have the new job

Write a sample starter sentence:

"Hello, Mr. Peterson. I'm really glad you hired me for this job, and I can't wait to get started!"

Starter Sentence Worksheet

Person: _____

Time & Place: _____

What are some of his/her interests or topics you want to talk about?

Write a sample starter sentence:

Person: _____

Time & Place: _____

What are some of his/her interests or topics you want to talk about?

Write a sample starter sentence:

Starter Sentence Worksheet

Person:_____

Time & Place: _____

What are some of his/her interests or topics you want to talk about?

Write a sample starter sentence:

Person:_____

Time & Place: _____

What are some of his/her interests or topics you want to talk about?

Write a sample starter sentence:

Starter Sentence Worksheet

Person:_____

Time & Place: _____

What are some of his/her interests or topics you want to talk about?

Write a sample starter sentence:

Person:_____

Time & Place: _____

What are some of his/her interests or topics you want to talk about?

Write a sample starter sentence:

5 Participating in a Reciprocal Conversation

Having a conversation with someone is a reciprocal activity. This means that *words are exchanged* between two or more people.

When people play a game of catch, they toss a ball back and forth to each other several times. *Having a reciprocal conversation is a lot like playing a game of catch.* You and the other person will talk about a specific topic "back and forth" as if you are throwing and catching words and thoughts between each other.

Usually two people will have a topic of conversation that they talk about for a little while. While one person speaks by making a comment or asking a question about the topic, the other person listens and waits for his/her turn. Then the second person gets a chance to make a comment or ask a question about the *same topic.*

The topic of conversation usually gets "tossed" back and forth *at least three times.* If both people really like the topic, they may "toss" the conversation back more than three times until they run out of things to say about the topic.

Topic Toss

Topics are usually tossed back and forth **at least three times.**
Practice following through on a topic by filling in the blanks
with appropriate conversation about the main topic.

Topic: _Weather_

Do you think it will rain today?

Toss

I was just outside, and it's sunny and warm. I don't think it will rain.

Toss

That's good because I was hoping to play soccer after school!

Topic Toss

Topics are usually tossed back and forth **at least three times.**
Practice following through on a topic by filling in the blanks
with appropriate conversation about the main topic.

Topic:_____

Toss

Toss

Topic Toss

Topics are usually tossed back and forth **at least three times.**
Practice following through on a topic by filling in the blanks
with appropriate conversation about the main topic.

Topic:_____

44

Topic Toss

Topics are usually tossed back and forth **at least three times.**
Practice following through on a topic by filling in the blanks
with appropriate conversation about the main topic.

Topic:_____

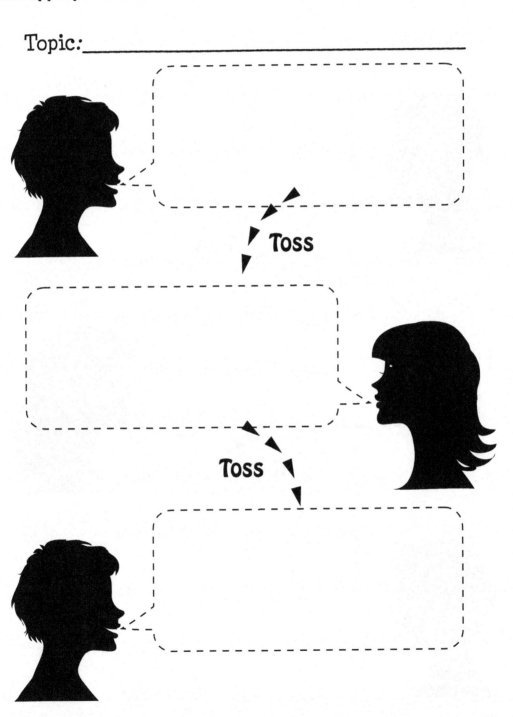

Topic Toss

Topics are usually tossed back and forth **at least three times.**
Practice following through on a topic by filling in the blanks
with appropriate conversation about the main topic.

Topic:_____

Toss

Toss

QUIZ TIME!

1. Reciprocal conversation means that words and ideas are _____ between two or more people.

2. Having a reciprocal conversation is like playing a game of _____.

3. During a reciprocal conversation, one person _____ while the other people are listening and waiting their turn.

4. A topic of conversation usually is "tossed" back and forth at least _____ times.

5. People having a reciprocal conversation may change topics when they run out of _____ to say about a topic.

6 Paying Attention & Listening to Others

Listening is the key to understanding other people. If someone is talking but no one is listening, there is no real communication going on.

It is important to recognize that not only should you "hear" the words they are speaking, you should also focus and process what they are saying. This is called "active listening" because your brain is actively engaged in the communication process.

People may not be comfortable if you stand too close during a conversation. A good rule of thumb is to position yourself one arm's length away from the other people with whom you are conversing.

Four important social skills that are expected of people when they are engaged in conversation:

 1 When someone is talking, I should stand and face towards him/her.

WHY?

I should stand facing towards someone so that I can hear clearly and let him/her know that I am **paying attention**.

2 I should look at the face of the person who is talking to me.

WHY?

I should look at the face of the person that is talking to me so that he/she knows that I am **listening**.

3 When someone is talking, I should look directly into his/her eyes occasionally.

WHY?

If I occasionally look into the other person's eyes during the conversation, we will both feel **"connected"** to the conversation.

4 When someone is talking to me, I should acknowledge that I am listening by nodding my head or making a brief comment about what he/she is saying.

WHY?

I should acknowledge what someone is saying by nodding or making a comment so that the other person knows that I understand **what is being said**.

QUIZ TIME!

List four important social behaviors that are expected when you are listening to other people talk:

 _____

 _____

 _____

 _____

Add TWO more social behaviors that you feel are important for people to display during a conversation. (For example, don't stare off into space when the other person is speaking)

 _____

 _____

STORY TIME

Have you ever felt frustrated because people were not listening to what you were saying? Write a story about what happened and how it made you feel.

_____

_____

_____

_____

_____

_____

_____

_____

_____

_____

_____

_____

_____

_____

_____

_____

_____

_____

_____

_____

_____

7 Responding to Questions

It is important to respond when someone asks you a question. People usually ask questions because they need information from you or want your opinion on a topic, so it is important to respond. It helps the other person understand why you are thinking of doing something or what you need from him/her.

Even if you think the person asking the question already knows the answer, it is still necessary to answer the question. Believe it or not, he/she may not know the answer or may have forgotten the information. Sometimes it can be difficult to remember everything and asking you is a good way to make sure the other person has the details right.

List three reasons you should respond to others on the next page. Then try to think of some questions that other people have asked you recently, list your response to them, and indicate how they acted after you responded. If they showed confusion or irritation, you probably did not respond to their question in the way they expected. How would you change that if asked the same question by the same people?

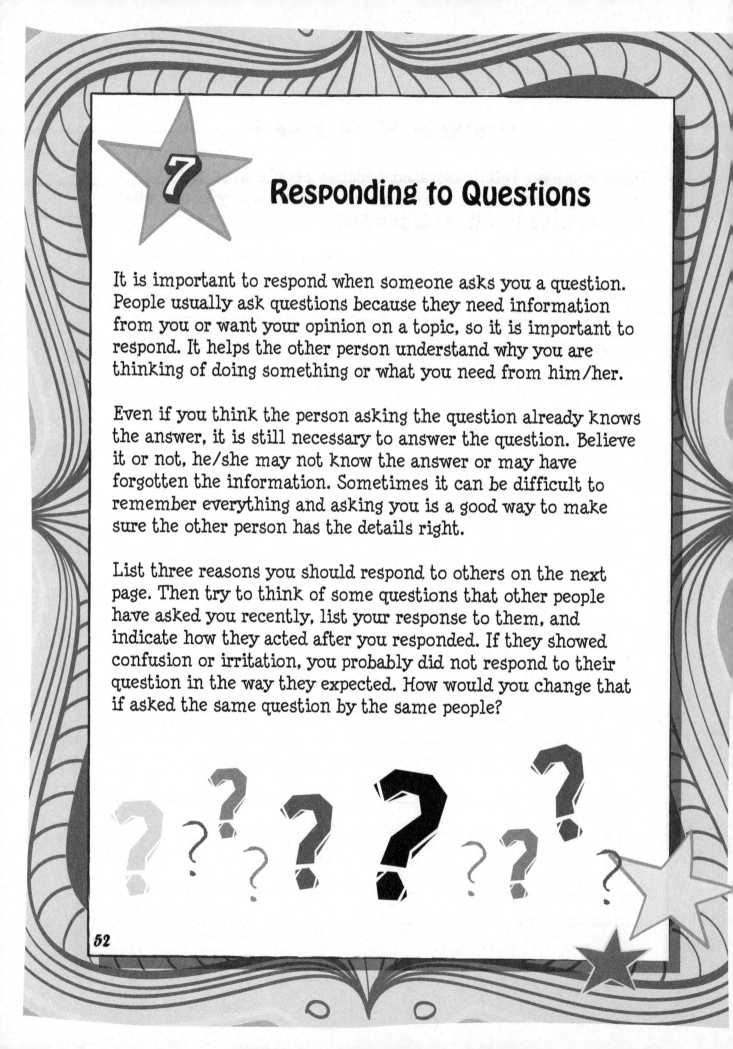

List three reasons to respond when others ask you questions...

1.

2.

3.

Use this form to evaluate specific situations in which you responded to questions. Was your response a good one? Think about what you will do differently the next time.

Who: _Mom_

Time & Place: _At home after school_

The question was:
Mom asked me if I had given Mrs. Fields the signed field trip persmission form today.

My response was:
I had forgotten to do it, so I yelled at her and ran upstairs to my room.

This was a GOOD / (BAD) response because:
I was mad at myself because I forgot, so I lost my temper and was angry with my Mom for asking me about it.

What will I do differently next time?
I will stay CALM and tell my Mom that I forgot to do it today, but will remember to give the form to the teacher tomorrow before class.

Use this form to evaluate specific situations in which you responded to questions. Was your response a good one? Think about what you will do differently the next time.

Who: _____

Time & Place: _____

The question was:

_____

_____

_____

My response was:

_____

_____

_____

_____

This was a GOOD / BAD response because:

_____

_____

_____

_____

What will I do differently next time?

_____

_____

_____

_____

Use this form to evaluate specific situations in which you responded to questions. Was your response a good one? Think about what you will do differently the next time.

Who: _____

Time & Place: _____

The question was:

_____

_____

_____

My response was:

_____

_____

_____

_____

This was a GOOD / BAD response because:

_____

_____

_____

_____

What will I do differently next time?

_____

_____

_____

_____

Use this form to evaluate specific situations in which you responded to questions. Was your response a good one? Think about what you will do differently the next time.

Who: _____

Time & Place: _____

The question was:

_____

_____

_____

My response was:

_____

_____

_____

_____

This was a GOOD / BAD response because:

_____

_____

_____

What will I do differently next time?

_____

_____

_____

Voice & Volume Control

8

Your voice is unique. It has a sound like nothing else. It also has the ability to go from a very soft, quiet level to a very loud level. If you talk too quietly, it can be difficult for people to hear or understand what you are saying. But if you talk too loudly, it can bother other people and make it difficult for them to listen to you.

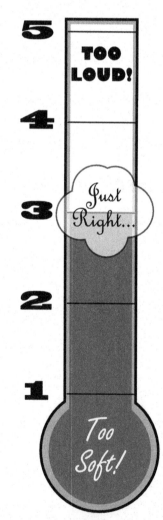

5

TOO LOUD!

4

Just Right...

3

2

1

Too Soft!

It is important to have good voice control. This means that you try to keep the loudness of your voice at a good level. Sometimes, it helps to think of your voice as a thermometer. When you are calm and cool, your voice volume is low. But as you become upset or excited, your voice volume tends to rise just like a thermometer.

You also may need to raise or lower your volume in different environments. For example, you will need to speak louder at a football game just to be heard and much softer in a quiet place like a library.

It is helpful to practice having good volume control. **Develop a "signal" with your parent or teacher so that when your voice is getting too loud or too soft, he/she can "signal" you.** This will help you to know how to adjust your voice to an appropriate volume level.

Color in the thermometer to show the appropriate level of volume for each situation:

5 4 3 2 1

School Cafeteria

5 4 3 2 1

Movie Theater

5 4 3 2 1

Classroom

Now list a place you are going to be today under each thermometer and color in the the appropriate level of volume for each situation:

5 4 3 2 1

5 4 3 2 1

5 4 3 2 1

_____   _____   _____

Waiting Your Turn To Speak

We have already learned that conversations are like games of catch. While one person is talking, the other person is listening and receiving the information. Then it is the other person's turn to talk.

When kids are young, they often have difficulty waiting their turn to speak. Many kids will interrupt others while they are talking, which is considered rude. But adults generally overlook such behavior in small children because they understand that making mistakes is part of the learning process.

As kids grow and mature, they are expected to be able to control themselves and interruptions are less tolerated. It can be very aggravating talking to a person who is constantly interrupting.

Interrupting is not only considered inappropriate but it also makes it difficult for both the speaker and the interrupter to follow the conversation. This will affect your ability to understand what is being said and your ability to think about what your response should be to the comments or questions from the person who is talking.

QUIZ TIME!

It is important to wait your turn to talk so that you can...

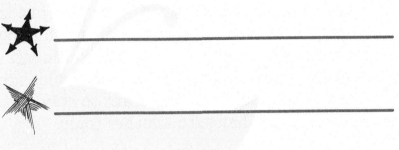

If you talk while another person is talking, the following things may happen...

Staying on Topic & Switching Topics

When people are having a conversation, they pick one topic to discuss at a time. They will usually talk about this topic for a while and give each other a chance to make comments or ask questions about the topic. You will find some topics more interesting than others, but it is important to stay on topic until it is appropriate to change to another topic.

When everyone is done talking about one topic, they will then begin to talk about something different. This is called "switching topics." Having a conversation with someone about a topic is kind of like following a path together. You are following a path in your minds together by thinking about the same topic and focusing on comments that are being made. When someone 'switches topics', he or she is 'changing the path'. This forces the other person in the conversation to switch paths also.

A starting topic may be something general, like weather, and used primarily to get the conversation going, not to express important ideas. While it may not be discussed as long as other topics, it is still a good idea to bounce the topic back and forth at least three times before switching to a topic that may be of more interest to you. Switching paths is ONLY okay if everyone is ready to talk about something else.

You usually make a transitional statement on the current topic before switching to a new topic. For example, in the topic toss on page 42, one person transitions from the topic of "weather" to the new topic "soccer" by saying that he hopes the weather will be good enough to play soccer after school.

QUIZ TIME!

Complete the sentences below:

1. When people have a conversation, they pick a
_____ to discuss.

2. During a conversation, all people involved
should have a chance to make a
_____ or ask a _____
about the topic being discussed.

3. Having a conversation about a specific topic is
kind of like following a _____
with the other person since you are both
focusing on the same thing at the same time.

4. When people in the conversation
_____ topics, they are changing the
"path" they are on.

5. Changing paths is okay if everyone involved
in the conversation is ready to talk
about_____ else.

11 Respecting the Ideas of Others

People are unique and different. That is what makes us all so interesting. It is important to understand that in a given situation not everyone is having the same thoughts as you are. This is usually because of some of the following:

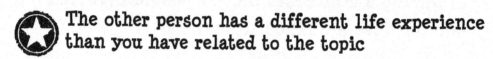 The other person has a different life experience than you have related to the topic

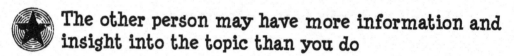 The other person may have more information and insight into the topic than you do

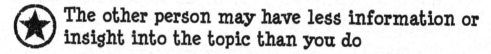 The other person may have less information or insight into the topic than you do

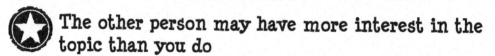 The other person may have more interest in the topic than you do

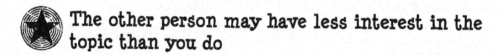 The other person may have less interest in the topic than you do

Even people that you have a lot in common with may have a difference of opinion from you occasionally. This is okay. You don't have to agree with everyone about everything; however, you should be accepting that other people have a difference of opinion about a given topic.

It is important to accept that someone has a different viewpoint but it does not mean that you have to compromise your own. Sometimes the best thing to say is, "Let's agree to disagree" and then change the topic.

Respecting the ideas of others
T-CHART

Everyone will not always agree with you. Use this T-Chart to plan what you WILL DO and WILL NOT do when this situation arises. *(Hint: We've filled in a few to get you started.)*

What I can do or say if someone has a difference of opinion...	**What I should NOT do or say if someone has a difference of opinion...**
-listen to what they are saying	-look away from them
-Say "I appreciate that you have a different point of view, but I think... (state your view point)	-roll your eyes

Ending a Conversation

Friendly conversations are structured like books or stories because they have a **beginning, middle** and **ending** to them. It is important to end a conversation with another person appropriately so that you are being polite.

Below are some examples of good and bad ways to end a conversation:

DO wait for the other person to stop talking. (If they continue talking without pausing to let you reply, you may say "Excuse me...")

DO look at them and smile and say something like "It's been nice talking to you, but I have to go now."

DO NOT just walk away without saying anything. Abruptly leaving in the middle of a conversation would be very rude.

DO NOT say "I'm bored with this conversation." That would most likely hurt the other person's feelings.

EXIT STRATEGIES...

Practice makes perfect! Write down how you would deal with this situation, then read the correct answer below. (Yes, it's upside down!)

Your friend Zoe is telling you about her new baby sister. The problem is that she has been talking about her sister non-stop for weeks, and you are BORED of the subject. How can you end the conversation without hurting her feelings?

_____

_____

_____

_____

_____

_____

_____

_____

_____

_____

_____

_____

_____

_____

Correct Answer: Having a new baby sister is a new and exciting experience for Zoe, and she probably doesn't realize that other people don't share her enthusiasm. If you have listened politely and bounced this subject back and forth a few times already, it's perfectly reasonable to change the subject. You could say" "I hope your little sister will like soccer when she grows up. By the way, did you see the same on TV last night?"

EXIT STRATEGIES...

Practice makes perfect! Write down how you would deal with this situation, then read the correct answer below. (Yes, it's upside down!)

You are talking to your music teacher after school about whether you should try out for concert band. You suddenly remember that your Mom was going to pick you up early this afternoon and she's been waiting for five minutes already. You should...

_____

_____

_____

_____

_____

_____

_____

_____

_____

_____

_____

_____

_____

_____

_____

Correct Answer: Although it is rude to end a conversation abruptly, sometimes it just can't be avoided. The most polite thing to do would be to wait for a break in the conversation, and then say; "Pardon me, but I just remembered that my Mom is waiting outside for me. May we continue this conversation tomorrow?" Your teacher will most likely respond with "Of course! Don't keep your Mom waiting. We will chat again tomorrow."

EXIT STRATEGIES...

Now it's your turn! Think of a situation you may be faced with in the future and write your own "Exit Strategy" below:

The Situation:

_____
_____
_____
_____
_____
_____
_____
_____

The Exit Strategy:

_____
_____
_____
_____
_____
_____
_____
_____
_____
_____
_____
_____
_____
_____

EXIT STRATEGIES...

Now it's your turn! Think of a situation you may be faced with in the future and write your own "Exit Strategy" below:

The Situation:

_____

_____

_____

_____

_____

_____

_____

_____

The Exit Strategy:

_____

_____

_____

_____

_____

_____

_____

_____

_____

_____

_____

_____

_____

_____

EXIT STRATEGIES...

Now it's your turn! Think of a situation you may be faced with in the future and write your own "Exit Strategy" below:

The Situation:

_____
_____
_____
_____
_____
_____
_____
_____

The Exit Strategy:

_____
_____
_____
_____
_____
_____
_____
_____
_____
_____
_____
_____
_____

13 Your Notes...

Attached are pages for you to use daily to track your conversation skills. Before you meet someone, plan how to approach him/her, what you will say, and how you will keep the conversation moving. Some of this will have to be spontaneous, but you can use the previous exercises to get ideas of what will happen and how to prepare.

After a conversation, take time to write down your thoughts on how it went. Did you feel anxious or comfortable? Did you enjoy any part of it and why or why not? Take each of the below areas and break down your conversation into what happened with each part.

The more you look back on each conversation and understand what worked and what did not, the more comfortable and skilled you will become in conversations.

Thoughts for your notes...

1 What topics were discussed?

2 Who started the conversation and what words did he/she use to start it?

3 Did everyone take equal turns talking or did some people talk more than the others?

4 Did everyone pay attention to what others were saying?

5 Did each person respond appropriately when asked a question?

6 Did everyone wait their turn to speak and if not, did people interrupt others often? How did a person respond when interrupted?

7 Did everyone stay on topic except when it was appropriate to switch to a new topic? How often did the topic switch? (and were the transitions smooth?)

8 Who ended the conversation and what words did he/she use to do that? Were you ready for the conversation to end if you weren't the one to end it?

Date: _____

Time: _____

Notes:

_____
_____
_____
_____
_____
_____
_____
_____
_____
_____
_____
_____
_____
_____
_____
_____
_____
_____
_____
_____
_____
_____

Date: _____

Time: _____

Notes:

_____

_____

_____

_____

_____

_____

_____

_____

_____

_____

_____

_____

_____

_____

_____

_____

_____

_____

_____

_____

_____

_____

_____

Date: _____

Time: _____

Notes:

_____

_____

_____

_____

_____

_____

_____

_____

_____

_____

_____

_____

_____

_____

_____

_____

_____

_____

_____

_____

_____

Date: _____

Time: _____

Notes:

_____
_____
_____
_____
_____
_____
_____
_____
_____
_____
_____
_____
_____
_____
_____
_____
_____
_____
_____
_____
_____
_____
_____
_____
_____

Date: _____

Time: _____

Notes:

_____

_____

_____

_____

_____

_____

_____

_____

_____

_____

_____

_____

_____

_____

_____

_____

_____

_____

_____

_____

_____

_____

Date: _____

Time: _____

Notes:

_____

_____

_____

_____

_____

_____

_____

_____

_____

_____

_____

_____

_____

_____

_____

_____

_____

_____

_____

_____

_____

_____

_____

_____

_____

Date: _____

Time: _____

Notes:

_____

_____

_____

_____

_____

_____

_____

_____

_____

_____

_____

_____

_____

_____

_____

_____

_____

_____

_____

_____

_____

Date: _____

Time: _____

Notes:

Date: _____

Time: _____

Notes:

_____
_____
_____
_____
_____
_____
_____
_____
_____
_____
_____
_____
_____
_____
_____
_____
_____
_____
_____
_____
_____
_____

Date: _____

Time: _____

Notes:

_____
_____
_____
_____
_____
_____
_____
_____
_____
_____
_____
_____
_____
_____
_____
_____
_____
_____
_____
_____
_____
_____
_____

Date: _____

Time: _____

Notes:

_____

_____

_____

_____

_____

_____

_____

_____

_____

_____

_____

_____

_____

_____

_____

_____

_____

_____

_____

_____

_____

_____

Date: _____

Time: _____

Notes:

_____

_____

_____

_____

_____

_____

_____

_____

_____

_____

_____

_____

_____

_____

_____

_____

_____

_____

_____

_____

_____

_____

_____

_____

_____

_____

Date: _____

Time: _____

Notes:

_____

_____

_____

_____

_____

_____

_____

_____

_____

_____

_____

_____

_____

_____

_____

_____

_____

_____

_____

_____

_____

_____

Date: _____

Time: _____

Notes:

_____

_____

_____

_____

_____

_____

_____

_____

_____

_____

_____

_____

_____

_____

_____

_____

_____

_____

_____

_____

_____

_____

Date: _____

Time: _____

Notes:

_____
_____
_____
_____
_____
_____
_____
_____
_____
_____
_____
_____
_____
_____
_____
_____
_____
_____
_____
_____
_____
_____
_____
_____
_____

Date: _____

Time: _____

Notes:

89

Date: _____

Time: _____

Notes:

_____

_____

_____

_____

_____

_____

_____

_____

_____

_____

_____

_____

_____

_____

_____

_____

_____

_____

_____

_____

_____

_____

Date: _____

Time: _____

Notes:

_____

_____

_____

_____

_____

_____

_____

_____

_____

_____

_____

_____

_____

_____

_____

_____

_____

_____

_____

_____

_____

_____

Date: _____

Time: _____

Notes:

_____

_____

_____

_____

_____

_____

_____

_____

_____

_____

_____

_____

_____

_____

_____

_____

_____

_____

_____

_____

_____

Date: _____

Time: _____

Notes:

_____

_____

_____

_____

_____

_____

_____

_____

_____

_____

_____

_____

_____

_____

_____

_____

_____

_____

_____

_____

_____

_____

_____

_____

_____

_____

Date: _____

Time: _____

Notes:

_____

_____

_____

_____

_____

_____

_____

_____

_____

_____

_____

_____

_____

_____

_____

_____

_____

_____

_____

_____

_____

_____

Date: _____

Time: _____

Notes:

_____

_____

_____

_____

_____

_____

_____

_____

_____

_____

_____

_____

_____

_____

_____

_____

_____

_____

_____

_____

_____

_____

_____

_____

_____

Date: _____

Time: _____

Notes:

_____

_____

_____

_____

_____

_____

_____

_____

_____

_____

_____

_____

_____

_____

_____

_____

_____

_____

_____

_____

_____

_____

_____

_____

Date: _____

Time: _____

Notes:

_____

_____

_____

_____

_____

_____

_____

_____

_____

_____

_____

_____

_____

_____

_____

_____

_____

_____

_____

_____

_____

_____

Date: _____

Time: _____

Notes:

_____

_____

_____

_____

_____

_____

_____

_____

_____

_____

_____

_____

_____

_____

_____

_____

_____

_____

_____

_____

_____

_____

_____

_____

Date: _____

Time: _____

Notes:

Date: _____

Time: _____

Notes:

_____

_____

_____

_____

_____

_____

_____

_____

_____

_____

_____

_____

_____

_____

_____

_____

_____

_____

_____

_____

_____

Date: _____

Time: _____

Notes:

_____

_____

_____

_____

_____

_____

_____

_____

_____

_____

_____

_____

_____

_____

_____

_____

_____

_____

_____

_____

_____

_____

Date: _____

Time: _____

Notes:

_____

_____

_____

_____

_____

_____

_____

_____

_____

_____

_____

_____

_____

_____

_____

_____

_____

_____

_____

_____

Date: _____

Time: _____

Notes:

_____

_____

_____

_____

_____

_____

_____

_____

_____

_____

_____

_____

_____

_____

_____

_____

_____

_____

_____

_____

_____

_____

_____

_____

Date: _____

Time: _____

Notes:

_____

_____

_____

_____

_____

_____

_____

_____

_____

_____

_____

_____

_____

_____

_____

_____

_____

_____

_____

_____

Date: _____

Time: _____

Notes:

_____

_____

_____

_____

_____

_____

_____

_____

_____

_____

_____

_____

_____

_____

_____

_____

_____

_____

_____

_____

_____

_____

_____

Date: _____

Time: _____

Notes:

_____

_____

_____

_____

_____

_____

_____

_____

_____

_____

_____

_____

_____

_____

_____

_____

_____

_____

_____

_____

_____

Date: _____

Time: _____

Notes:

_____

_____

_____

_____

_____

_____

_____

_____

_____

_____

_____

_____

_____

_____

_____

_____

_____

_____

_____

_____

_____

_____

_____

_____

Date: _____

Time: _____

Notes:

_____

_____

_____

_____

_____

_____

_____

_____

_____

_____

_____

_____

_____

_____

_____

_____

_____

_____

_____

_____

Date: _____

Time: _____

Notes:

_____

_____

_____

_____

_____

_____

_____

_____

_____

_____

_____

_____

_____

_____

_____

_____

_____

_____

_____

_____

_____

_____

_____

Date: _____

Time: _____

Notes:

_____

_____

_____

_____

_____

_____

_____

_____

_____

_____

_____

_____

_____

_____

_____

_____

_____

_____

_____

_____

_____

Date: _____

Time: _____

Notes:

_____

_____

_____

_____

_____

_____

_____

_____

_____

_____

_____

_____

_____

_____

_____

_____

_____

_____

_____

_____

_____

_____

Date: _____

Time: _____

Notes:

_____

_____

_____

_____

_____

_____

_____

_____

_____

_____

_____

_____

_____

_____

_____

_____

_____

_____

_____

_____

_____

Date: _____

Time: _____

Notes:

_____

_____

_____

_____

_____

_____

_____

_____

_____

_____

_____

_____

_____

_____

_____

_____

_____

_____

_____

_____

_____

Date: _____

Time: _____

Notes:

_____
_____
_____
_____
_____
_____
_____
_____
_____
_____
_____
_____
_____
_____
_____
_____
_____
_____
_____
_____
_____
_____
_____
_____
_____

Date: _____

Time: _____

Notes:

_____

_____

_____

_____

_____

_____

_____

_____

_____

_____

_____

_____

_____

_____

_____

_____

_____

_____

_____

_____

_____

_____

_____

_____

_____

Date: _____

Time: _____

Notes:

_____

_____

_____

_____

_____

_____

_____

_____

_____

_____

_____

_____

_____

_____

_____

_____

_____

_____

_____

_____

_____